THE ROYAL HORTICULTURAL SOCIETY

WILD IN THE
GARDEN

DIARY
2023

Inspiring everyone to grow

First published in 2022 by Frances Lincoln Publishing,
an imprint of The Quarto Group.
The Old Brewery, 6 Blundell Street
London, N7 9BH, United Kingdom
www.Quarto.com

With thanks to Helen Bostock, RHS Senior Horticultural
Advisor, and Andrew Salisbury, RHS Principal Scientist
Entomology plant health.

RHS FLOWER SHOWS 2023

The Royal Horticultural Society holds a number of
prestigious flower shows throughout the year. At the
time of going to press, show dates for 2023 had not been
confirmed but details can be found on the website at:
rhs.org.uk/shows-events.

Every effort is made to ensure calendarial data is correct
at the time of going to press but the publisher cannot
accept any liability for any errors or changes.

Front cover: Bumblebee (*Bombus* spp.)
Back cover: Tawny owl (*Strix aluco*)

PICTURE CREDITS

CALENDAR 2023

JANUARY	FEBRUARY	MARCH	APRIL

JANUARY

M	T	W	T	F	S	S
						1
2	3	4	5	6	7	8
9	10	11	12	13	14	15
16	17	18	19	20	21	22
23	24	25	26	27	28	29
30	31					

FEBRUARY

M	T	W	T	F	S	S
		1	2	3	4	5
6	7	8	9	10	11	12
13	14	15	16	17	18	19
20	21	22	23	24	25	26
27	28					

MARCH

M	T	W	T	F	S	S
		1	2	3	4	5
6	7	8	9	10	11	12
13	14	15	16	17	18	19
20	21	22	23	24	25	26
27	28	29	30	31		

APRIL

M	T	W	T	F	S	S
					1	2
3	4	5	6	7	8	9
10	11	12	13	14	15	16
17	18	19	20	21	22	23
24	25	26	27	28	29	30

MAY

M	T	W	T	F	S	S
1	2	3	4	5	6	7
8	9	10	11	12	13	14
15	16	17	18	19	20	21
22	23	24	25	26	27	28
29	30	31				

JUNE

M	T	W	T	F	S	S
			1	2	3	4
5	6	7	8	9	10	11
12	13	14	15	16	17	18
19	20	21	22	23	24	25
26	27	28	29	30		

JULY

M	T	W	T	F	S	S
					1	2
3	4	5	6	7	8	9
10	11	12	13	14	15	16
17	18	19	20	21	22	23
24	25	26	27	28	29	30
31						

AUGUST

M	T	W	T	F	S	S
	1	2	3	4	5	6
7	8	9	10	11	12	13
14	15	16	17	18	10	20
21	22	23	24	25	26	27
28	29	30	31			

SEPTEMBER

M	T	W	T	F	S	S
				1	2	3
4	5	6	7	8	9	10
11	12	13	14	15	16	17
18	19	20	21	22	23	24
25	26	27	28	29	30	

OCTOBER

M	T	W	T	F	S	S
						1
2	3	4	5	6	7	8
9	10	11	12	13	14	15
16	17	18	19	20	21	22
23	24	25	26	27	28	29
30	31					

NOVEMBER

M	T	W	T	F	S	S
		1	2	3	4	5
6	7	8	9	10	11	12
13	14	15	16	17	18	19
20	21	22	23	24	25	26
27	28	29	30			

DECEMBER

M	T	W	T	F	S	S
				1	2	3
4	5	6	7	8	9	10
11	12	13	14	15	16	17
18	19	20	21	22	23	24
25	26	27	28	29	30	31

CALENDAR 2024

JANUARY

M	T	W	T	F	S	S
1	2	3	4	5	6	7
8	9	10	11	12	13	14
15	16	17	18	19	20	21
22	23	24	25	26	27	28
29	30	31				

FEBRUARY

M	T	W	T	F	S	S
			1	2	3	4
5	6	7	8	9	10	11
12	13	14	15	16	17	18
19	20	21	22	23	24	25
26	27	28	29			

MARCH

M	T	W	T	F	S	S
				1	2	3
4	5	6	7	8	9	10
11	12	13	14	15	16	17
18	19	20	21	22	23	24
25	26	27	28	29	30	31

APRIL

M	T	W	T	F	S	S
1	2	3	4	5	6	7
8	9	10	11	12	13	14
15	16	17	18	19	20	21
22	23	24	25	26	27	28
29	30					

MAY

M	T	W	T	F	S	S
	1	2	3	4	5	
6	7	8	9	10	11	12
13	14	15	16	17	18	19
20	21	22	23	24	25	26
27	28	29	30	31		

JUNE

M	T	W	T	F	S	S
					1	2
3	4	5	6	7	8	9
10	11	12	13	14	15	16
17	18	19	20	21	22	23
24	25	26	27	28	29	30

JULY

M	T	W	T	F	S	S
1	2	3	4	5	6	7
8	9	10	11	12	13	14
15	16	17	18	19	20	21
22	23	24	25	26	27	28
29	30	31				

AUGUST

M	T	W	T	F	S	S
			1	2	3	4
5	6	7	8	9	10	11
12	13	14	15	16	17	18
19	20	21	22	23	24	25
26	27	28	29	30	31	

SEPTEMBER

M	T	W	T	F	S	S
						1
2	3	4	5	6	7	8
9	10	11	12	13	14	15
16	17	18	19	20	21	22
23	24	25	26	27	28	29
30						

OCTOBER

M	T	W	T	F	S	S
	1	2	3	4	5	6
7	8	9	10	11	12	13
14	15	16	17	18	19	20
21	22	23	24	25	26	27
28	29	30	31			

NOVEMBER

M	T	W	T	F	S	S
				1	2	3
4	5	6	7	8	9	10
11	12	13	14	15	16	17
18	19	20	21	22	23	24
25	26	27	28	29	30	

DECEMBER

M	T	W	T	F	S	S
						1
2	3	4	5	6	7	8
9	10	11	12	13	14	15
16	17	18	19	20	21	22
23	24	25	26	27	28	29
30	31					

GARDENS AND WILDLIFE

Gardens are an important ecosystem. All ecosystems are interdependent and dynamic systems of living organisms interacting with the physical environment. Gardens by their nature are extremely variable, with a diversity of plants that can surpass that of 'natural' ecosystems. Combined with resources such as ponds and compost heaps, gardens deliver a wide variety of habitats where wildlife can thrive. Gardens provide food and a home for hundreds of creatures throughout their lifecycles, and this wildlife is vital to a healthy and vibrant living garden.

The large range of garden wildlife is there because of gardening, not despite it. Gardens provide resources year-round, from overwintering sites to summer food plants. No garden or green space is too small to provide some benefit. A window box, for instance, can provide a nectar stop for bumblebees and other pollinators. The huge range of plants and kinds of garden management results in a mosaic of habitats spanning a much wider area than a single garden. Wildlife doesn't recognise our boundaries and gardens provide important corridors enabling the movement of mammals such as hedgehogs, birds, butterflies and other creatures.

Most gardens already support a variety of wildlife and, with a little thought and planning, they can sustain even more. Adding more plants, a pond, bird, bee and bat boxes, decaying wood, a compost heap or an undisturbed leaf pile will provide valuable habitats. The more diverse the habitats, the greater the number of species of birds, bees, bats, beetles, moths and other natural creatures that will use a garden. The RHS recognises and actively promotes the valuable contribution that wildlife makes to gardens and gardens to wildlife. The act of gardening for wildlife can also bring great enjoyment and health benefits to gardeners. For more information visit: **www.rhs.org.uk** and **www.wildaboutgardens.org**

Red Admiral (*Vanessa atalanta*)

'Good hygiene is essential to prevent diseases, so clean the bird bath regularly.'

JOBS FOR THE MONTH

- Scatter bird food on the ground and bird table. Birds follow a routine, so replenish this regularly.
- Make sure that the water in the bird bath does not freeze over, and that it is cleaned regularly.
- If you have a pond and it freezes over, ensure that water is accessible by melting a hole at the water's edge.
- Hang bird feeders and fat balls on branches and fences, and keep them topped up.

BIRDS

- You can buy high-quality bird food from online or retail outlets. Alternatively, you can make your own fat balls using natural fats such as lard and beef suet. Fat from cooking, unsaturated margarines and vegetable oil are not suitable.
- In the winter, it is more important than ever to feed the birds in your garden, as many natural food sources such as seeds and berries are exhausted by this time.
- Placing food on wire mesh positioned just off the ground will encourage ground-feeding birds such as robins and dunnocks.
- If possible, try to keep your feeding regime consistent – this will encourage birds to regularly return to the garden.
- Common birds to see in winter include blackbirds, robins, blackcaps, tits and thrushes. Look out for redwings and fieldfares, too.

BIRD TABLES AND FEEDERS

You can protect birds from predators by positioning your bird table or feeders away from any areas easily accessed by cats. Cats can approach via roofs, trees or fences. Placing your feeders next to prickly bushes can be a good deterrent. Your bird table can be a simple tray, with or without a roof. It is advisable to avoid fancy designs that are difficult to clean. A raised edge will retain food, and a gap in each corner will allow water to drain away and help with cleaning. Move your bird feeders around the garden regularly to avoid damaging the ground underneath.

DECEMBER & JANUARY

Monday **26**

Tuesday **27**

Wednesday **28**

Thursday **29**

First quarter

Friday **30**

New Year's Eve

Saturday **31**

New Year's Day

Sunday **1**

JANUARY

2 *Monday*

3 *Tuesday*

Holiday, Scotland and New Zealand

4 *Wednesday*

5 *Thursday*

6 *Friday*

Full moon
Epiphany

7 *Saturday*

8 *Sunday*

Greenfinch (*Chloris chloris*) between two goldfinches (*Carduelis carduelis*)

JANUARY

Monday 9

Tuesday 10

Wednesday 11

Thursday 12

Friday 13

Saturday 14

Last quarter

Sunday 15

Leveret or young brown hare (*Lepus europaeus*)

JANUARY

16 *Monday* 												Holiday, USA (Martin Luther King Jnr Day)

17 *Tuesday*

18 *Wednesday*

19 *Thursday*

20 *Friday*

21 *Saturday* 												*New moon*

22 *Sunday* 												Chinese New Year

Blue tit (*Cyanistes caeruleus*)

JANUARY

Monday **23**

Tuesday **24**

Wednesday **25**

Holiday, Australia (Australia Day)

Thursday **26**

Friday **27**

First quarter

Saturday **28**

Sunday **29**

Seven-spot ladybird (*Coccinella septempunctata*)

JANUARY & FEBRUARY

30 *Monday*

31 *Tuesday*

1 *Wednesday*

2 *Thursday*

3 *Friday*

4 *Saturday*

5 *Sunday*
Full moon

'Even the smallest pond will attract birds, insects, newts, toads and frogs.'

BUILDING A POND

Late winter is a great time to put in a garden pond; you may get your first frogs and toads by spring. Even the smallest pond will attract birds, insects, newts, toads and frogs, while also providing an important water source. Here are some tips for adding a pond to your garden:

- Choose a bright, sunny location with at least one sloping side to provide easy access in and out of the water.
- Try planting around the edges of the pond or letting grass grow long to create a safe passage for animals to enter and exit the pond.
- Connect your water butt so it will automatically fill the pond during heavy rain.
- Variety in the pond will support more diverse animal life, so try to vary the depth of the water to include shallow as well as deeper areas.
- It can be helpful to include a section at the pond margin with cobbles, gravel or stones to provide easy drinking spots for bees and other pollinators.

JOBS FOR THE MONTH

- Put up nest boxes for birds.
- Continue to put food out for birds and keep your feeders topped up. Avoid putting out more food than can be eaten in a few days, or large chunks of food.
- Birds still need to bathe regardless of the cold, so if possible, keep the bird bath topped up and free of ice.

HEDGEHOGS

It is a good idea to put out food and water for hedgehogs in the autumn when they are preparing for hibernation. They may also appreciate having some food left out for them at this time of year. During mild spells, they can emerge from hibernation to forage for food, before returning to their hiding places as the temperature drops. Only leave food out during the winter months if it is being taken, but continue to provide a source of clean, fresh water and be careful that it doesn't freeze over.

FEBRUARY

Accession of Queen Elizabeth II
Holiday, New Zealand (Waitangi Day)

Monday **6**

Tuesday **7**

Wednesday **8**

Thursday **9**

Friday **10**

Saturday **11**

Sunday **12**

Nuthatch (*Sitta europaea*)

FEBRUARY

13 *Monday*   *Last quarter*

14 *Tuesday*   Valentine's Day

15 *Wednesday*

16 *Thursday*

17 *Friday*

18 *Saturday*

19 *Sunday*

Common darter (*Sympetrum striolatum*)

FEBRUARY

New moon
Holiday, USA (Presidents' Day)

Monday **20**

Shrove Tuesday

Tuesday **21**

Ash Wednesday

Wednesday **22**

Thursday **23**

Friday **24**

Saturday **25**

Sunday **26**

Blackbird fledgling (*Turdus merula*)

FEBRUARY & MARCH

27 *Monday*

First quarter

28 *Tuesday*

1 *Wednesday*

St David's Day

2 *Thursday*

3 *Friday*

4 *Saturday*

5 *Sunday*

INSECTS

Insects and other invertebrates are crucial to your garden's natural balance. They are vital for nutrient recycling and helping to break down dead plant matter, while other insects are predatory and help to control those that feed on plants. Many flying insects are also pollinators. Ladybirds, spiders and other invertebrates find winter shelter in evergreen bushes and climbers, and among fallen leaves, dead stems and seedheads.

HABITATS AND SHELTER

- Now is a good time to consider building or buying a bee home for solitary bees such as mason bees to colonise in the spring.
- A pile of old logs or bricks can provide welcome shelter for insects and other small creatures.
- Nest boxes for birds should be hung 1-3m high on walls or trees and fitted with a metal entrance guard to protect them from predators. It's also a good idea to tilt the box forward slightly to prevent rain from entering it.
- Make sure any nest boxes face the north or east, as the sun's heat can make them uninhabitable.

'A pile of old logs or bricks can provide welcome shelter for insects and other small creatures.'

JOBS FOR THE MONTH

- Check for any garden hazards such as loose netting and uncovered drains.
- Create log and twig piles from prunings and felled trees to provide protection for invertebrates and debris for nests.
- Keep the bird bath clean and topped up.
- Make your pond more wildlife friendly (see Week 5).
- Put up nest boxes for birds.
- Continue to top up bird feeders. Whole peanuts should be placed in a metal mesh feeder as they can be a choking hazard for young birds.
- Look out for amphibian spawn in ponds. Frog spawn is usually in jelly-like clumps; toad spawn is in longer individual strands; and newt spawn is laid separately on pondweed stems.

MARCH

Monday **6**

Full moon

Tuesday **7**

Wednesday **8**

Thursday **9**

Friday **10**

Saturday **11**

Sunday **12**

Common weasel (*Mustela nivalis*)

MARCH

---

13 *Monday*   Commonwealth Day

---

14 *Tuesday*

---

15 *Wednesday*   *Last quarter*

---

16 *Thursday*

---

17 *Friday*   St Patrick's Day
Holiday, Republic of Ireland and Northern Ireland

---

18 *Saturday*

---

19 *Sunday*   Mothering Sunday, UK and Republic of Ireland

Honey bee (*Apis mellifera*)

MARCH

Vernal Equinox (Spring begins)   *Monday* **20**

New moon   *Tuesday* **21**

Wednesday **22**

First day of Ramadân (subject to sighting of the moon)   *Thursday* **23**

Friday **24**

Saturday **25**

British Summer Time begins   *Sunday* **26**

Feverfew (*Tanacetum parthenium*)

MARCH & APRIL

27 *Monday*

28 *Tuesday*

29 *Wednesday*   *First quarter*

30 *Thursday*

31 *Friday*

1 *Saturday*

2 *Sunday*   Palm Sunday

Common toad tadpoles (*Bufo bufo*)

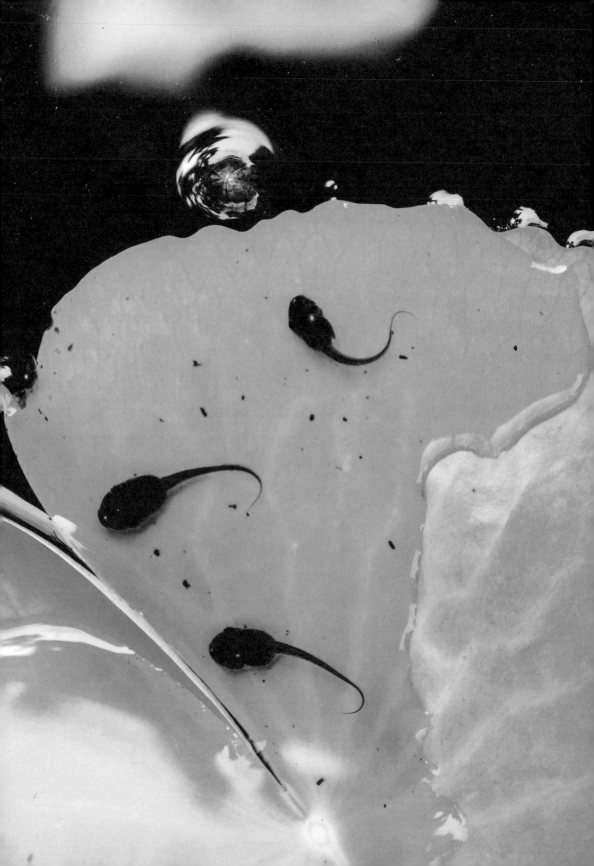

WAYS TO ENCOURAGE WILDLIFE

- Weed by hand as much as possible to avoid using herbicides, and remember to leave some 'weeds' such as dandelions in lawns, as they are a valuable source of nectar and pollen.
- Wildlife will use all areas of your garden but you may want to leave a patch where the grass is allowed to grow long or where disturbance is kept to a minimum, such as behind a shed.
- Stop mowing a chosen area of lawn to allow the grass and lawn flowers to grow. This will attract all sorts of grasshoppers, true bugs and many other insects.
- Build a compost heap for recycling organic garden waste. This will provide a habitat for a wide range of insects and other invertebrates.
- Mulch beds with garden compost or composted bark to feed earthworms and maintain a healthy living soil.
- Plants known to support a wide range of wildlife include honeysuckle, hawthorn, sunflowers and rowan trees.
- Replacing a fence with a mixed hedge will provide a safe 'corridor' for wildlife to move along, as well as nesting sites and food sources for small mammals, birds and a wide range of other animal life.

'Plant annuals and perennials to encourage pollinators into the garden.'

JOBS FOR THE MONTH

- Plant a hanging basket or window box to attract bees and butterflies using nasturtiums, English marigolds and lavender. Make sure to position it somewhere sunny.
- Plant annuals and perennials (single flowers as opposed to double flowers) to encourage pollinators into the garden. You can look for those on the RHS Plants for Pollinators lists.
- Keep the bird bath and feeders clean and topped up. Put out additional food on the ground.
- Remove excess plant growth from ponds, leaving it on the side for twenty-four hours before adding it to the compost heap to allow any trapped creatures to return to the water.
- Make or buy a bat box and mount it on a sheltered but sunny wall.

APRIL

Monday 3

Tuesday 4

Wednesday 5

Full moon
Maundy Thursday
First day of Passover (Pesach)

Thursday 6

Good Friday
Holiday, UK, Canada, Australia and New Zealand

Friday 7

Saturday 8

Easter Sunday

Sunday 9

APRIL

10 *Monday*

11 *Tuesday*

12 *Wednesday*

13 *Thursday*   *Last quarter*

14 *Friday*

15 *Saturday*

16 *Sunday*

Orange-tip butterfly (*Anthocharis cardamines*)

Monday **17**

Tuesday **18**

Wednesday **19**

New moon

Thursday **20**

Eid al-Fitr (end of Ramadân) (subject to sighting of the moon)
Birthday of Queen Elizabeth II

Friday **21**

Saturday **22**

St George's Day

Sunday **23**

Banded demoiselle dragonfly (*Calopteryx splendens*)

APRIL

24 *Monday*

25 *Tuesday*   Holiday, Australia and New Zealand (Anzac Day)

26 *Wednesday*

27 *Thursday*   *First quarter*

28 *Friday*

29 *Saturday*

30 *Sunday*

Common frog (*Rana temporaria*)

BATS

- Bats are excellent pest controllers. All bats are legally protected in Britain and this extends to their roosting and hibernation sites.
- There are 17 species of bat breeding in Britain, but their numbers have declined. The more common species to see in the garden are the common and soprano pipistrelle, brown long-eared, noctule and Daubenton's.
- Bats eat flying insects at night, including mosquitoes, moths and beetles, helping to keep garden pests at bay.
- Garden ponds and night-flowering plants such as evening primrose encourage the types of insects that bats like to hunt.
- Now is a good time to make or buy a bat box and mount it as high as possible on a sheltered sunny wall. Avoid positions close to security lights and keep garden lighting to a minimum.
- Other common roosting sites include eaves or behind weatherboarding on the south face of buildings.
- During the day bats hide in dark places like hollow trees, so retain old trees with cavities in the trunk, where possible.
- Late summer is the best time for bat watching in the evening.

'Bats are a good indication of a healthy, insect-rich environment.'

JOBS FOR THE MONTH

- Be careful to avoid disturbing nesting birds, and never cut a hedge or shrub if you suspect birds are present.
- Leave informal hedges untrimmed to provide food and shelter for wildlife.
- Continue to top up and clean out the bird bath and feeders.
- Sowing annuals such as cosmos, phacelia and cornflowers will attract insects, as will allowing some of your plants to go to seed.
- Create log, twig and rock piles to create shelter for wildlife.
- Mow a path through any areas of long grass and pull out any weeds in areas sown with annual flower mixes.

BIRDS

By this time of the year, migrant birds will have arrived from Africa, such as swifts and swallows. The dawn chorus can be deafening as birds compete for territories and mates. Swallows and spotted flycatchers will nest on suitable ledges in or on quiet outbuildings.

MAY

Monday **1**

Early Spring Bank Holiday, UK
Holiday, Republic of Ireland

Tuesday **2**

Wednesday **3**

Thursday **4**

Friday **5**

Full moon

Saturday **6**

Sunday **7**

MAY

8 *Monday*

9 *Tuesday*

10 *Wednesday*

11 *Thursday*

12 *Friday*   *Last quarter*

13 *Saturday*

14 *Sunday*   Mother's Day, USA, Canada, Australia and New Zealand

Great spotted woodpecker (*Dendrocopos major*)

MAY

Monday **15**

Tuesday **16**

Wednesday **17**

Ascension Day
Thursday **18**

New moon
Friday **19**

Saturday **20**

Sunday **21**

Red squirrel (*Sciurus vulgaris*)

MAY

22 *Monday*   Holiday, Canada (Victoria Day)

23 *Tuesday*

24 *Wednesday*

25 *Thursday*

26 *Friday*   Feast of Weeks (Shavuot)

27 *Saturday*   *First quarter*

28 *Sunday*   Whit Sunday

Bumblebee (*Bombus* spp.)

JOBS FOR THE MONTH

- Make a bee drinker out of a plant saucer filled with pebbles and water.
- Thin out, cut back or divide excessive new growth on aquatic plants, making sure to leave the cuttings by the side of the pond for a while before transferring them to the compost heap.
- Allow herbs such as marjoram, mint and sage to flower to encourage bees and butterflies.
- Where slugs are a problem, try to use an organic slug control.
- Continue to put out food for birds regularly.
- Allow your lawn to grow longer, letting some lawn flowers bloom. Avoiding the use of lawn weedkillers will allow insect life to thrive.
- Avoid pruning hip-producing roses – these are a useful source of food for wildlife.

MAMMALS

Many creatures are raising young at this time of year and young mammals are beginning to explore the world beyond their homes. Hedgehogs in particular are very active, with litters usually being born in June or July. You may see or hear their parents foraging for food at night.

'Avoiding the use of lawn weedkillers will allow insect life to thrive.'

MAKE AN UPCYCLED CONTAINER POND

You can upcycle an old plastic container to make a wildlife-friendly container pond.

- Position your container somewhere that catches a little sun, but where it won't be in the sun all day as this can warm the water up too much or cause it to evaporate too quickly.
- If the container leaks, you can use a sheet of pond liner to make it watertight, securing it in place with a silicone-based sealer.
- Make your container pond wildlife friendly by creating a ramp so that frogs and other wildlife can get in and out. A stack of stones, bricks or logs can all work well.
- Fill your container with rainwater.
- Gently lower in a mix of floating and upright pond plants. For a mini-pond, three to five plants is usually enough. They may look small to start with, but they can grow very quickly.

MAY & JUNE

Spring Bank Holiday, UK
Holiday, USA (Memorial Day)

Monday 29

Tuesday 30

Wednesday 31

Thursday 1

Coronation Day

Friday 2

Saturday 3

Full moon
Trinity Sunday

Sunday 4

JUNE

5 *Monday*

Holiday, Republic of Ireland
Holiday, New Zealand (The Queen's Birthday)

6 *Tuesday*

7 *Wednesday*

8 *Thursday*

Corpus Christi

9 *Friday*

10 *Saturday*

Last quarter
The Queen's Official Birthday (subject to confirmation)

11 *Sunday*

Rose chafer (*Cetonia aurata*) on barberry (*Berberis*) flowers

JUNE

Holiday, Australia (The Queen's Birthday)

Monday **12**

Tuesday **13**

Wednesday **14**

Thursday **15**

Friday **16**

Saturday **17**

Sunday **18**

New moon
Father's Day, UK, Republic of Ireland, USA and Canada

Six-spot burnet (*Zygaena filipendulae*)

JUNE

19 *Monday*   Holiday, USA (Juneteenth)

20 *Tuesday*

21 *Wednesday*   Summer solstice (Summer begins)

22 *Thursday*

23 *Friday*

24 *Saturday*

25 *Sunday*

Chaffinch (*Fringilla coelebs*)

INSECTS

Summer is flying ant season, so look out for these in the garden. There is also an abundance of hoverflies at this time of year. Adult hoverflies are pollinators and the larvae of many species feed on greenfly and other aphids. Wasps can also be good pest controllers, as well as being useful flower pollinators.

CHOOSING BIRD FOOD

If you want to encourage a particular species of bird into your garden, try leaving out food particular to their requirements.

- **Wrens** prefer natural foods but will take fat and seed
- **Starlings** peanut cakes
- **Dunnocks** fat and small seeds on the ground
- **Robins** live mealworms
- **Finches** berry cakes
- **Goldfinches** niger seeds
- **Sparrows, finches and nuthatches** sunflower heads
- **Thrushes and blackbirds** fruit such as over-ripe apples, raisins and songbird mix scattered on the ground
- **Tits** insect cakes

JOBS FOR THE MONTH

- Put out hedgehog food and check that holes in the bottom of fences haven't become blocked, so hedgehogs can freely move between gardens.
- Construct a hedgehog feeding station for the garden.
- Delay hedge trimming until the end of summer to allow wildlife to nest, shelter and feed in them. You should also leave nesting birds undisturbed in garden shrubs and trees.
- Keep your bird feeders topped up.
- Top up ponds and water features if necessary, ideally using stored rainwater.
- Remove dead foliage and blooms from aquatic plants. Leave at the side of the pond for a while to allow wildlife to return to the water before adding them to the compost heap.
- Avoid deadheading roses that produce hips, as these are a valuable food source.
- Watch out for young frogs and newts leaving the pond as they begin to move further afield.

First quarter

Monday 26

Tuesday 27

Wednesday 28

Thursday 29

Friday 30

Canada Day

Saturday 1

Sunday 2

JULY

---

3 *Monday*

Full moon
Holiday, Canada (Canada Day)

---

4 *Tuesday*

Holiday, USA (Independence Day)

---

5 *Wednesday*

---

6 *Thursday*

---

7 *Friday*

---

8 *Saturday*

---

9 *Sunday*

Harvest mouse (*Micromys minutus*)

JULY

Last quarter   *Monday* **10**

Tuesday **11**

Battle of the Boyne
Holiday, Northern Ireland   *Wednesday* **12**

Thursday **13**

Friday **14**

St Swithin's Day   *Saturday* **15**

Sunday **16**

European rabbit (*Oryctolagus cuniculus*)

JULY

---

17 *Monday*   *New moon*

---

18 *Tuesday*

---

19 *Wednesday*   Islamic New Year

---

20 *Thursday*

---

21 *Friday*

---

22 *Saturday*

---

23 *Sunday*

A garden mix of cornfield annuals, including cornflowers (*Centaurea cyanus*) and poppies (*Papaver rhoeas*)

JULY

Monday 24

First quarter   *Tuesday* 25

Wednesday 26

Thursday 27

Friday 28

Saturday 29

Sunday 30

Jay (*Garrulus glandarius*)

JULY & AUGUST

31 *Monday*

1 *Tuesday*   *Full moon*

2 *Wednesday*

3 *Thursday*

4 *Friday*

5 *Saturday*

6 *Sunday*

'Leave some windfall apples, pears and plums for birds to feed on.'

BIRDS

- Many adult birds fly fairly low in late summer, hiding in cool, shady places while their feathers are replaced during the summer moult.
- August sees the departure of swifts, although the majority of other migrant bird species can still be found in the garden. Starlings, jackdaws and house sparrows, in particular, can be seen caring for their young in the nest.
- Birdsong may be reduced or less obvious this month, and young birds can be seen exploring their environment.
- In hot, dry weather many birds enjoy 'dust-bathing' as well as splashing about in the bird bath.
- A way to supplement natural habitats is to install or build a nest box to encourage birds to your garden. The main criteria are that the nest box is weatherproof, safe and secure.

JOBS FOR THE MONTH

- Continue to top up bird feeders and put food on bird tables and on the ground. Leave some windfall apples, pears and plums for birds to feed on.
- Dead head flowers to encourage them to produce more blooms and pollen for insects.
- Allow seedheads to develop on some plants as a food source. Don't trim any bushes with developing berries, such as holly, cotoneaster and pyracantha.
- Leave fledglings undisturbed if you find them on the ground – their parents are probably not far away.
- Plant marigolds around the vegetable patch to attract hoverflies for pest control.
- Continue putting out food and water for hedgehogs.

IN THE GARDEN

- Bumblebees, solitary bees and hoverflies are busy collecting nectar and pollen from flowers and herb gardens.
- Butterflies, including the summer migrant Painted Lady, flock to buddleja.
- Bats can be spotted flying at night, hunting for insects.
- Grey squirrels can be heard chattering and squealing at one another while chasing each other around the treetops.

AUGUST

Holiday, Scotland and Republic of Ireland

Monday **7**

Last quarter

Tuesday **8**

Wednesday **9**

Thursday **10**

Friday **11**

Saturday **12**

Sunday **13**

Cinnabar moth caterpillar (*Tyria jacobaeae*)

AUGUST

14 *Monday*

15 *Tuesday*

16 *Wednesday*   *New moon*

17 *Thursday*

18 *Friday*

19 *Saturday*

20 *Sunday*

Eurasian badger (*Meles meles*)

AUGUST

Monday **21**

Tuesday **22**

Wednesday **23**

First quarter   *Thursday* **24**

Friday **25**

Saturday **26**

Sunday **27**

Great tit (*Parus major*)

AUGUST & SEPTEMBER

28 *Monday*   Summer Bank Holiday, UK (exc. Scotland)

29 *Tuesday*

30 *Wednesday*

31 *Thursday*   *Full moon*

1 *Friday*

2 *Saturday*

3 *Sunday*   Father's Day, Australia and New Zealand

'To support butterflies, you need to look after the caterpillars in your garden.'

BUTTERFLIES

Some of the most common butterflies to see in the garden are Red Admiral, Painted Lady, Comma, Brimstone, Peacock, Green-veined White, Small White and Large White. You may sometimes see Orange-tip, Speckled Wood, Meadow Brown, Small Copper and Holly Blue. The Small Tortoiseshell used to be commonly seen but its numbers have declined in recent years. Here are some ways you can encourage butterflies to your garden:

- In late summer, butterflies like Red Admiral and Painted Lady will appreciate fallen fruit left on the ground.
- Adult butterflies feed on nectar so plant a range of nectar-rich flowers such as red valerian and asters to flower from March through to October–November.
- To support butterflies, you need to look after the caterpillars in your garden, so research which plants will best support them. For example, ivy and holly support both caterpillars and adult Holly Blue butterflies.

JOBS FOR THE MONTH

- As we come to the end of the nesting season, hedge trimming can resume – but delay for another month if you suspect birds are still active.
- Hedgehogs can benefit from supplementary feeding in the autumn, helping them to survive winter. Give them special hedgehog food, or dog or cat food, but never bread and milk.
- Cover the pond surface with netting to stop excessive amounts of fallen leaves from getting in.
- Give meadows a final cut before winter. Leave the clippings to lie for a couple of days before removing. This will allow wildflower seeds to fall to the ground and replenish the meadow.
- Create piles of logs, twigs or rocks to create shelter for wildlife.

SPIDERS

Spiders have an important role to play in an ecologically balanced garden. They eat many other invertebrates and can be food for birds, forming part of the garden's diverse food web. To encourage spiders, try to use pesticides as little as possible and plant tall flowers and dense bushes to create 'scaffolding' for spiders to build their webs on.

SEPTEMBER

Holiday, USA (Labor Day)
Holiday, Canada (Labour Day)

Monday **4**

Tuesday **5**

Last quarter

Wednesday **6**

Thursday **7**

Friday **8**

Saturday **9**

Sunday **10**

Peacock butterfly (*Aglais io*)

SEPTEMBER

11 *Monday*

12 *Tuesday*

13 *Wednesday*

14 *Thursday*

15 *Friday*   *New moon*

16 *Saturday*   Jewish New Year (Rosh Hashanah)

17 *Sunday*

Water vole (*Arvicola terrestris*)

SEPTEMBER

Monday **18**

Tuesday **19**

Wednesday **20**

Thursday **21**

First quarter

Friday **22**

Autumnal Equinox (Autumn begins)

Saturday **23**

Sunday **24**

Long-tailed tit (*Aegithalos caudatus*)

SEPTEMBER & OCTOBER

25 *Monday*   Day of Atonement (Yom Kippur)

26 *Tuesday*

27 *Wednesday*

28 *Thursday*

29 *Friday*   Full moon
Michaelmas Day

30 *Saturday*   First day of Tabernacles (Succoth)

1 *Sunday*

'Be careful when turning over compost heaps, as small animals may be sheltering there.'

IN THE GARDEN

- Winter migrant birds start to arrive from colder, northern regions. Starlings gather in large groups.
- Look out for redwings, bramblings and fieldfares, but don't be surprised if your feeder is untouched. Birds will still be foraging for natural food, such as holly berries.
- Avoid disturbing butterflies such as Red Admirals which overwinter in garden buildings.
- Many butterflies, including Small Tortoiseshell, are still about, along with hoverflies and ladybirds.
- Some moth caterpillars such as angleshades can be found feeding throughout the year. Although caterpillars eat plants, they should be tolerated when possible, as they form a part of a healthy, balanced garden.
- Some food for butterfly caterpillars in gardens include ivy, holly, hops, nasturtium, thistle, buckthorn and blackthorn.

JOBS FOR THE MONTH

- Make a leaf pile for hibernating mammals and overwintering ground-feeding birds; add in some logs to widen the appeal for a greater range of insects.
- Build a 'bug hotel' using bundles of twigs or hollow stems.
- If possible, allow uncut ivy to flower as it is an excellent late nectar source for pollinating insects and the berries last well into winter to feed birds.
- Leave herbaceous and hollow stemmed plants unpruned until early spring to provide homes for overwintering insects.
- Top up bird feeders and put food out on the ground and bird tables. Whole peanuts are safe, as the breeding season is now over.
- Clean the bird bath regularly and ensure that it is topped up with fresh water.
- Where possible, leave seedheads standing to provide food and shelter for wildlife.
- Be careful when turning over compost heaps, as frogs, toads and other small animals may be sheltering there.
- Autumn daisies are a good source of food for butterflies and bees, particularly when there are few other plants for them to feed on.

OCTOBER

Monday 2

Tuesday 3

Wednesday 4

Thursday 5

Last quarter

Friday 6

Saturday 7

Sunday 8

Tawny owl (*Strix aluco*)

OCTOBER

9 *Monday*

10 *Tuesday*

11 *Wednesday*

12 *Thursday*

13 *Friday*

14 *Saturday*

New moon

15 *Sunday*

Common lizard (*Zootoca vivipara*)

OCTOBER

Monday 16

Tuesday 17

Wednesday 18

Thursday 19

Friday 20

Saturday 21

First quarter

Sunday 22

Dunnock (*Prunella modularis*)

OCTOBER

23 *Monday*   Holiday, New Zealand (Labour Day)

24 *Tuesday*

25 *Wednesday*

26 *Thursday*

27 *Friday*

28 *Saturday*   *Full moon*

29 *Sunday*   British Summer Time ends

Hawthorn (*Crataegus monogyna*)

'Consider options other than a bonfire for disposing of garden waste.'

JOBS FOR THE MONTH

- Make a leaf pile for hibernating mammals and retain fallen leaves at the base of hedges for blackbirds and thrushes to hunt through for invertebrates.
- Empty and clean out nest boxes using boiling water. When they are thoroughly dry, place a handful of wood shavings inside to provide winter shelter.
- Animals still need access to water for drinking, so melt a hole in ice at the edge of a pond by filling a saucepan with hot water and sitting it on the ice until a hole has melted. Never crack or hit the ice as the shock waves created can harm wildlife.
- Now is the time to make sure you are putting out high fat foods for birds, such as peanut cake and fat balls.
- Consider options other than a bonfire for disposing of garden waste. If you do have a bonfire, always check for animals before lighting.

MOTHS

There are more than 2,500 species of moths in Britain and they play an important role in all ecosystems, including healthy gardens. Adult moths and their caterpillars are a key food source for many animals such as hedgehogs, spiders, frogs, bats and birds. Day-flying and night-flying moths act as plant pollinators.

POND CARE

- Regularly shake off leaves from protective nets over ponds. Remove any leaves that are not caught by the net.
- Conserve water and connect your water butt so that it fills the pond automatically during heavy rain.
- Encourage newts to breed by introducing some non-invasive, submerged, aquatic plants into the pond. Newts lay their eggs on narrow-leaved plants.

OCTOBER & NOVEMBER

Holiday, Republic of Ireland | *Monday* **30**

Halloween | *Tuesday* **31**

All Saints' Day | *Wednesday* **1**

| *Thursday* **2**

| *Friday* **3**

| *Saturday* **4**

Last quarter
Guy Fawkes Night | *Sunday* **5**

NOVEMBER

6 *Monday*

7 *Tuesday*

8 *Wednesday*

9 *Thursday*

10 *Friday*   Holiday, USA (Veterans Day)

11 *Saturday*   Veterans Day, USA
Remembrance Day, Canada

12 *Sunday*   Remembrance Sunday

Eurasian otter (*Lutra lutra*)

NOVEMBER

New moon

Monday **13**

Tuesday **14**

Wednesday **15**

Thursday **16**

Friday **17**

Saturday **18**

Sunday **19**

Goldcrest (*Regulus regulus*)

NOVEMBER

20 *Monday*   *First quarter*

---

21 *Tuesday*

---

22 *Wednesday*

---

23 *Thursday*   Holiday, USA (Thanksgiving)

---

24 *Friday*

---

25 *Saturday*

---

26 *Sunday*

Red squirrel (*Sciurus vulgaris*)

'Holly berries are a valuable food source for birds, so think twice before using them for Christmas decorations.'

PLANT FOR WILDLIFE

- Building a range of habitats will support the needs of a variety of creatures along the food chain.
- Key features to consider including are lawn, trees, shrubs, flowers and water.
- Planting a single tree provides a host of habitats for a wide variety of insects and other animals. Native trees can be especially good for wildlife, but always match the tree to the space as some may get too large or not be suited to urban conditions.
- Prune your shrubs at different times to create varied cycles of growth to benefit wildlife.
- Create micro-habitats such as small patches of grass to allow birds easy access to grubs and worms. Long grass creates habitats for egg-laying and overwintering insects; a pile of logs will provide shelter for small animals.
- Consider planting more shrubs and trees that produce berries, as these will provide a valuable food source for birds.

JOBS FOR THE MONTH

- Keep the bird bath topped up, clean and ice-free.
- Top up bird feeders and put food out on the ground and bird tables. Wrens and other small birds appreciate finely chopped bacon rind and grated cheese.
- Mulch vegetable beds with garden compost but delay cutting back borders until late winter, to provide shelter for invertebrates.
- Plant hedges, single-flowered roses and fruit trees to offer plenty of resources for wildlife, including blossom and fruit.
- Holly berries are a valuable food source for birds, so think twice before using them in any Christmas decorations.
- Take care when pruning, as butterflies and moths overwinter in places that are sheltered from wind, frost and rain. They favour a thick tangle of leaves and stems, but some will use sheds or garages.

NOVEMBER & DECEMBER

Full moon

Monday 27

Tuesday 28

Wednesday 29

St Andrew's Day

Thursday 30

Friday 1

Saturday 2

First Sunday in Advent

Sunday 3

DECEMBER

4 *Monday*

5 *Tuesday*   *Last quarter*

6 *Wednesday*

7 *Thursday*   Hannukah begins (at sunset)

8 *Friday*

9 *Saturday*

10 *Sunday*

Goldfinch (*Carduelis carduelis*)

DECEMBER

Monday 11

New moon   *Tuesday* 12

Wednesday 13

Thursday 14

Hannukah ends   *Friday* 15

Saturday 16

Sunday 17

Red fox (*Vulpes vulpes*)

DECEMBER

18 *Monday*

19 *Tuesday*   *First quarter*

20 *Wednesday*

21 *Thursday*

22 *Friday*   Winter Solstice (Winter begins)

23 *Saturday*

24 *Sunday*   Christmas Eve

European hedgehog (*Erinaceus europaeus*)

DECEMBER

Christmas Day
Holiday, UK, Republic of Ireland, USA,
Canada, Australia and New Zealand

Monday **25**

Boxing Day (St Stephen's Day)
Holiday, UK, Republic of Ireland, USA,
Canada, Australia and New Zealand

Tuesday **26**

Full moon

Wednesday **27**

Thursday **28**

Friday **29**

Saturday **30**

New Year's Eve

Sunday **31**

European robin (*Erithacus rubecula*)

YEAR PLANNER

JANUARY	JULY
FEBRUARY	AUGUST
MARCH	SEPTEMBER
APRIL	OCTOBER
MAY	NOVEMBER
JUNE	DECEMBER